Michael Winicott

I0488655

JESUS CHRIST: LEADERSHIP LESSONS

Learning from One of History's Greatest Leaders

Published by UNITEXTO

UNITEXTO
Digital Publishing

TABLE OF CONTENTS

INTRODUCTION

Born in the humblest of circumstances, Jesus of Nazareth would go on to change the world. For today's leaders, for whom the study of leadership is often a natural part of the calling, Jesus is an understandably compelling figure.

The fact is that Jesus' teachings do not always jibe or mesh comfortably with conventional wisdom, particularly as expressed in the popular leadership books of the day, and that this is part of what makes them so valuable.

Jesus was a leader of the highest order, and his perspectives on leadership and the realizing of human potential are as fresh and vital today as they must have been all those centuries ago.

Leaders who commit to really understanding and giving consideration to what Jesus has to say will find the task as rewarding as it is challenging.

As a spiritual leader who sought to deliver flawed human beings to the Kingdom of Heaven, Jesus aimed far higher than most, playing with the sorts of stakes that dwarf those of mundane life today.

To give such an inimitable, effective leader his due, then, is to look beyond the surface of what he is saying, and to pursue the deeper truth that is always waiting beneath.

One of the most demanding and inspiring teachers and leaders of all time, Jesus has plenty to offer to those who are willing to accept the challenges he offers and who genuinely seek to appreciate his distinctive way of leading others to make the most of themselves.

THE LIFE AND TIMES OF JESUS OF NAZARETH IN BRIEF

Most of what can be said today about Jesus' life comes from the four Synoptic Gospels of the Christian Bible's New Testament, so-called because, taken together, they provide the best available synopsis of his years on Earth. After the well-known episode of his miraculous birth in a manger to his virgin mother Mary, an event detailed in the Gospels of Luke and Matthew, nothing more is said in the canonical books of the Bible about his childhood at all.

Instead, the Biblical accounts of Jesus' life pick back up decades later, where he is reintroduced as a mature carpenter or wood worker, a characterization that is also prominent in the historical records of the early Christian Church. Jesus is depicted as requesting baptism at the hands of John the Baptist, an itinerant Jewish prophet of the time who was one of the most influential and well-known throughout the region.

The Gospel of Matthew says that, as the far-seeing John looked on to what he saw as the fulfillment of one of his own prophesies, the Holy Spirit descended upon Jesus at that moment, elevating him from human nature and setting him on the well-known path that followed.

After fasting for forty days and fighting off the temptations and challenges set before him by Satan, Jesus embarked upon his ministry proper, gathering about him a group of twelve disciples whom he would eventually anoint as the Apostles who would spread his teachings after he was gone. Wandering around Galilee and the area around Jerusalem, Jesus delivered sermons and personal lessons to gatherings of all sorts, as well as his disciples, becoming better known as he and his followers traveled the countryside.

Eventually, after the famous events in the Temple of Jerusalem, Jesus was betrayed by his own disciple Judas. Foreseeing that his life on Earth was at an end, Jesus sought to prepare his disciples for his departure, once again reinforcing in a most concrete way at the Last Supper the lessons in humility and sacrifice that he had taught to them.

The Gospels of Luke, Mark, and Matthew state that, before Jesus was arrested and crucified as punishment for his challenging the social order of the day, he was once again pointed out as the Messenger of God, with his Transfiguration being witnessed by three of his closest disciples. The Gospels say that Jesus was resurrected after finally succumbing to the ravages of the Cross, with his followers discovering an empty tomb where he had been laid to rest. The resurrected Jesus then made a final appeal to his disciples that they should spread his teachings as far and wide as they could, before being taken up to Heaven.

In fact, through their efforts and those of the Apostle Paul, a former persecutor of Christians who was converted as he walked the road to Damascus, Jesus' teachings would spread first throughout the region and eventually the world. No leader of people today can fail to be impressed by how successful and powerful of a leader Jesus was, and he left behind a wealth of teachings that are just as valuable today as they were in his time, cutting directly, as so many of them do, to the eternal truths of human nature.

JESUS' 10 MOST IMPORTANT LEADERSHIP LESSONS

While Jesus' teachings are incredibly valuable for the leaders of today to consider and absorb, they can also be extremely challenging. That means that it is often fruitful to go beyond the first impression that his teachings can leave, and to think about the deeper, more fundamental point that he was driving at.

It is also frequently useful to pay close attention to Jesus' conduct as a committed, powerful leader himself. In fact, part of what has made the study of Jesus' life and teachings so valuable for leaders throughout the ages is this two-fold nature of what he has to offer. Both the particular lessons he imparts and the way he goes about doing that can often be of real, concrete value to leaders set on making the most of their own abilities.

Lesson 1: Improve yourself first
One especially striking thing about Jesus' teachings in the Bible is how frequently some of them crop up in different forms. Repetition was clearly a key part of his strategy for turning his disciples into the independent Apostles who would go on to spread his message after he was gone, with several themes standing out particularly in this respect.

Probably the most prominent of all of these repeated lessons was the idea that humans should resist the temptation to judge others, saving their energies for self-analysis and striving for self-improvement instead. One of the most famous passages from the New Testament makes this point head-on, in a way that is difficult to deny:

> Do not judge, or you too will be judged. For in the same way you judge others, you will be judged, and with the measure you use, it will be measured to you. Why do you look at the speck of sawdust in your brother's eye and pay no attention to the plank in your own eye? How can you say to your brother, 'Let me take the speck out of your eye,' when all the time there is a plank in your own eye? You hypocrite, first take the plank out of your own eye, and then you will see clearly to remove the speck from your brother's eye. (Matt. 7: 1-5, New International Version)

As with many of Jesus' teachings, this can be a difficult one to swallow for those who are most concerned with leadership. Leadership, after all, seems inevitably to entail judging others; how else can a leader hope to fruitfully direct a group of subordinates if not by making them aware of their flaws and showing them how to do better?

The important thing to remember here is that Jesus himself was a leader and, in fact, one of the greatest in all of history. Not only was he consciously showing his disciples and others how to be better people and prepare themselves for entry into the Kingdom of Heaven, he was also striving to ready those disciples for the moment when they, themselves, would need to do the same for others.

Even in this strikingly direct passage, Jesus does not simply forbid that a leader should judge others. He instead makes it clear that any such effort can only ultimately be successful if the leader has gone to great effort to recognize and deal with their own weaknesses first. This is made even more explicit in another of the New Testament's best-known passages:

> *Leave them; they are blind guides. If the blind lead the blind, both will fall into a pit.* (Matt. 15: 14, NIV)

It can be tempting for leaders, people who are naturally ambitious, energetic, and engaged with the world around them, to want to hit the ground running, to immerse themselves in everything as a way of taking charge and helping their organizations achieve greater things. Through these two passages, Jesus points out that there is a real need, though, for an equally dedicated attention to the leader's inner life.

Leaders who fail to root out and deal with their own weaknesses and blind spots, at the very least, cannot hope to help others do the same. In many cases, in fact, leaders who do not bother with the tough work of personal improvement and introspection are likely to lead their followers into trouble as a result.

This is a lesson that is conveyed throughout the Gospels in a number of different forms, all clearly pointing toward the same central point. The undeniable directive for today's leaders is that all who hope to succeed in the endeavor must be consistently dedicated to improving themselves, just as much as they are devoted to bringing out the best in others.

Lesson 2: Let Honors and Respect Find Their Way to You

Another notable thing about Jesus' teaching was how consistently he challenged his listeners and disciples. Even those of humble ambitions and self-image will find plenty to grapple with in his parables, aphorisms, and direct lessons. Those who aim higher in terms of achievement and worldly stature, then, are likely to find many of his teaching even more challenging.

One excellent example of this crops up in the Gospel of Luke, when Jesus dines with a number of Pharisees, a prominent social and political group of the time whose thinking eventually became the basis for much of today's Rabbinical Judaism. Alert to their guest's reputation, the Pharisees begin questioning him on points of Mosaic Law, seeking to trip him up.

As was his way, Jesus refuses to be drawn into the trap. Instead, he deftly parries their probes, finally responding with a story that undermines their entire effort, stopping them in their tracks:

> *When he noticed how the guests picked the places of honor at the table, he told them this parable: "When someone invites you to a wedding feast, do not take the place of honor, for a person more distinguished than you may have been invited. If so, the host who invited both of you will come and say to you, 'Give this person your seat.' Then, humiliated, you will have to take the least important place. But when you are invited, take the lowest place, so that when your host comes, he will say to you, 'Friend, move up to a better place.' Then you will be honored in the presence of all the other guests. For all those who exalt themselves will be humbled, and those who humble themselves will be exalted."* (Luke 14: 7-11, NIV)

Conscious of Jesus' prominence and his reputation for helping others understand Mosaic Law in a new and more edifying light, the Pharisees had sought to improve their own standing by conspicuously knocking him down a peg. Jesus points out the futility of this ambition in a plain but striking way, not only escaping the argumentative grasp of the Pharisees, but imparting a valuable lesson at the same time.

As with many of Jesus' teachings, there are at least two lessons here that modern leaders can do well to absorb. The first is the overt message of the parable: consciously, conspicuously striving for honors and respect is a good way to end up with the opposite. Instead, Jesus suggests, those who wish to be honored should focus on the hard, apparently humble work that might initially seem unrewarding.

While it can be tempting for those in leadership positions to tend toward self-aggrandizement and glory-hounding, this almost always backfires in the end. Leaders who come to command enduring respect instead typically do the opposite, putting thoughts of honors out of mind, and devoting themselves to what needs to be done. Respect comes to them naturally, over time, as others cannot help but recognize how much they have accomplished.

The other important lesson for leaders here is a subtler one that ties into the first. Confronted with a bald, direct challenge to his standing and authority, Jesus does not respond in kind. Someone who was obsessed with maintaining standing and respect might have been put off balance and left to lash out, achieving at best a stalemate with the challengers.

Instead, Jesus' command of himself allows him to parry the Pharisees' thrusts in an elegant, focused way that ultimately leaves everyone a winner. The second lesson from this passage, then, is one about Jesus' way of leadership, and it is one that is frequently in evidence throughout the Gospels. Only a person who has learned to see clearly, as in the lesson from the previous section of this book, and is not blinded by a need for immediate respect and honor can hope to lead so deftly.

Lesson 3: Lead by Serving
Time and time again throughout the Gospels, Jesus challenges the status quo, pointing out how the conventional convictions of his listeners can be dangerous and damaging. While today's world would hardly be recognizable, in many ways, to someone from the first century, the fact is that basic human nature has not changed since. That means that people today still make many of the same mistakes that others did back then and have just as much to learn from Jesus.

For example, despite being an extremely challenging, demanding leader, Jesus also distinguished himself through his lack of pomposity. Even being motivated by the grand ambition of helping his disciples find their way to the Kingdom of Heaven, he maintained a humble, dutiful attitude about his leadership, seeking to do whatever was right for them in every case.

He makes this point explicitly in the Gospel of Mark, clearly establishing his outlook and encouraging his disciples to adopt it as their own:

Jesus called them together and said, "You know that those who are regarded as rulers of the Gentiles lord it over them, and their high officials exercise authority over them. Not so with you. Instead, whoever wants to become great among you must be your servant, and whoever wants to be first must be slave of all. For even the Son of Man did not come to be served, but to serve, and to give his life as a ransom for many." (Mark 10: 42-45, NIV)

One of the greatest human leaders of all, then, saw the essence of his calling not as a matter of leading others but of serving them. That is not to say that Jesus did not consider himself a leader, but that he recognized the futility of focusing on leadership as an end in itself. He had an important goal, even the most important of all, and his leadership was a means toward that end.

He recognized this, in fact, in such a fundamental, concrete way that he could understand the essence of his leadership as being what most would consider the exact opposite. Jesus' leadership was a kind of servitude, an utter devotion to doing whatever was most needed for his disciples and others with whom he came into contact with. It was servitude so complete, as he says explicitly in this important passage from Mark, that it would culminate in his sacrificing his life for those he served and led.

This is an especially powerful and compelling lesson for leaders of all kinds today. In our modern, achievement-oriented society, leaders are rightly admired and celebrated, and this fact can tempt some to come to think of their leadership as something that is valuable in itself. In fact, as Jesus points out in such a powerful fashion, the most effective and committed leaders realize that their activities are far better understood in the context of a greater goal.

The most effective leaders embody this realization to the extent that their leadership efforts become what can only be seen as a kind of service to those they lead and to the greater projects they align themselves with. Leaders who succeed in the difficult task of conceiving of themselves and their work in this way free themselves of the energy-sapping, counter-productive distraction that comes with lording their leadership over others, as Jesus points out. True leadership is never an end in itself, and leaders who maintain the humility to see it as a kind of service can be the most effective of all.

Lesson 4: Recognize Valuable Mistakes
The Gospels are overflowing with parables so striking and touching that they have become a part of modern

culture at large, growing well beyond their great significance to those of the Christian faith. One of the most famous of all of these educational stories is that of the Prodigal Son, a tale of redemption and forgiveness that appeals to people around the world at a very basic level.

That story, whereby a wayward son, having squandered the inheritance he demanded, returns to his father not to receive condemnation but to be celebrated instead, is also an important one for modern leaders to absorb. There is an often-understandable focus in the modern corporate world on cutting loose those who have made costly mistakes. While this might often be the best course of action, a well-rounded leader, one who is capable of making the most of any situation, will also be able to recognize when such failings merit a more patient response or even praise:

> *"The son said to him, 'Father, I have sinned against heaven and against you. I am no longer worthy to be called your son.'*
>
> *"But the father said to his servants, 'Quick! Bring the best robe and put it on him. Put a ring on his finger and sandals on his feet. Bring the fattened calf and kill it. Let's have a feast and celebrate. For this son of mine was dead and is alive again; he was lost and is found.' So they began to celebrate.* (Luke 15: 21-24, NIV)

The Prodigal Son has not merely failed at establishing an independent life in the wider world. He has demanded and wasted a share of his father's hard work in the form of an early inheritance, leaving himself starving and desperate. Far from scorning him for his failures, the father in the story recognizes that his son has truly learned an important lesson. While it was a costly one for all concerned, his father has the presence of mind and calmness of purpose to realize that the lesson, ultimately, is a victory that should be celebrated.

The point of the story of the Prodigal Son, of course, is not that every failure should be rewarded or even accepted. The father in the parable here is not being a pushover; instead, he simply recognizes that this particular failure has an upside, and that all are ultimately better for it.

This can be a difficult lesson for leaders to put into practice, but it is an extremely important one. In the competitive atmosphere of today's business world, being overly soft on failure can be taken as a sign of weakness, of not having the stomach to make the tough decisions that leaders are responsible for.

A truly well-rounded, multidimensional leader, though, will be able to recognize those moments when the time is right for holding back. A well-known, but possibly apocryphal story, from IBM's corporate history has it that famed CEO Tom Watson, Jr., once summoned to his office an executive who had presided over a disastrous project that cost the company millions of dollars. Sure that he was to be fired, the executive was surprised to hear Watson instead say "Fire you? Not when I've just spent $10 million educating you."

It can be incredibly difficult for leaders to recognize when such tolerance is merited, and even more so to have the courage to act accordingly. The reality, though, is that some mistakes truly are valuable, and that acting otherwise can be just as damaging as tolerating failures that have no such upside. Once again, Jesus is demanding that his disciples look deeper, beyond their everyday habits and convictions, and seek out the underlying truth, an important lesson for today's leaders, as well.

Lesson 5: Appreciate Lower Perfomances and Contributions

The laser-like focus on achievement and top performers that often prevails in the highest echelons of today's organizations can do more than just cause leaders to overlook mistakes that are actually valuable. It can also cause many leaders to neglect an important kind of talent and dedication in their organizations, one that often sets the stage for the accomplishments of those who naturally attract praise and encouragement.

In an especially poignant passage of the Gospel of Mark known as "The Widow's Offering," Jesus calls attention to the value that contributions of an apparently humble sort can sometimes conceal:

> *Jesus sat down opposite the place where the offerings were put and watched the crowd putting their money into the temple treasury. Many rich people threw in large amounts. But a poor widow came and put in two very small copper coins, worth only a few cents.*
>
> *Calling his disciples to him, Jesus said, "Truly I tell you, this poor widow has put more into the treasury than all the others. They all gave out of their wealth; but she, out of her poverty, put in everything—all she had to live on".* (Mark 12: 41-44, NIV)

Every ambitious leader feels pressed for time, and this means that it can be tempting to focus almost exclusively on those members of an organization who stand out for their capabilities and achievements. Encouraging excellence in subordinates, of course, is an important task for every leader, and it is one that Jesus himself devoted a good portion of his life as a leader to.

That alone, though, is not enough, for truly effective leadership invariably also means recognizing and valuing the contributions of those who are less capable.

The impoverished widow in this parable gives all that she has at the temple, thereby making the kind of sacrifice, relative to her means, that richer people who contribute far more could never even contemplate.

The lesson here is not that today's leaders should encourage mediocrity or settle for it. It is that, in every organization, there will inevitably be some people who are simply not capable of standing with the top performers, and recognizing the value they provide is important. Far from being a merely cynical perspective, this is an absolute truism: Even in the organizations that are flushest with talent, there will be a gradation of capability within the ranks.

Leaders who excel accept this logical inevitability and strive to make the most of it. Instead of merely dismissing the contributions of those who fail to rise the highest, they look to see if these efforts represent all that the lower performers are capable of. When that turns out to be the case, the ablest leaders give credit where it is due, praising and encouraging these contributions for the effort and sacrifice that they represent.

The flip side of this lesson, of course, is that leaders should also be on the lookout for even those standout performers who refuse to give their all. Jesus does not suggest that the contributions of the temple's wealthy patrons should be dismissed, but he points out quite clearly that they represent far less in the way of commitment than the poor widow's does. While a naturally talented person who contributes a lot to an organization without trying much could well be valuable, a skilled leader will recognize this squandering of potential and work to do something about it.

As he frequently does, then, Jesus asks his disciples to look beyond surface appearances and delve into the true significance of things. Modern leaders who settle for the surface impressions that simple performance metrics and the like give rise to might thereby make their own jobs easier, but they are likely not doing all they can to make the most of their subordinates and organizations. Jesus' lesson is to look deeper, to work harder to figure out just what particular contributions really represent, and to act in accordance with what is discovered.

Lesson 6: Prepare the Ground for Success

Leaders are typically people who are naturally inclined to action, who instinctively forge ahead while others hesitate. In fact, this is often a valuable trait, and Jesus himself never seems prone to excessive prevarication in the Gospels.

The most effective leaders, though, couple this basic tendency toward action with a strategic, thoughtful outlook that helps to make the most of it. Jesus makes this point quite clearly in an extended passage in the Gospel of Matthew, using the image of a seed being sown that recurs frequently throughout the Bible:

> Then he told them many things in parables, saying: "A farmer went out to sow his seed. As he was scattering the seed, some fell along the path, and the birds came and ate it up. Some fell on rocky places, where it did not have much soil. It sprang up quickly, because the soil was shallow. But when the sun came up, the plants were scorched, and they withered because they had no root. Other seed fell among thorns, which grew up and choked the plants. Still other seed fell on good soil, where it produced a crop—a hundred, sixty or thirty times what was sown. (Matt. 13: 3-8, NIV)

While it is delivered in a metaphorical way, the point here is a clear one: Simply acting, even in a basically sensible way, is no guarantee of success. Better, instead, to take care to make the most of those actions by preparing beforehand and acting strategically, as part of a greater plan. Instead of wasting his stocks of seed by scattering them thoughtlessly, the farmer in the parable would have been better off focusing on the good soil that produced a reward many times what was sown in it.

In case this was not direct enough, Jesus lays things out in even finer detail for the large crowd that has gathered on the shore of a lake to listen to him as he preaches from a boat:

> *Listen then to what the parable of the sower means: When anyone hears the message about the kingdom and does not understand it, the evil one comes and snatches away what was sown in their heart. This is the seed sown along the path. The seed falling on rocky ground refers to someone who hears the word and at once receives it with joy. But since they have no root, they last only a short time. When trouble or persecution comes because of the word, they quickly fall away. The seed falling among the thorns refers to someone who hears the word, but the worries of this life and the deceitfulness of wealth choke the word, making it unfruitful. But the seed falling on good soil refers to someone who hears the word and understands it. This is the one who produces a crop, yielding a hundred, sixty or thirty times what was sown.* (Matt. 13: 18-23, NIV)

Once again, Jesus delivers a message that is of two-fold significance for today's leaders. On the more specific level, it speaks to the importance of preparing other people to make good use of the advice and leadership that is directed at them. Great leaders not only think about and hone their own skills, they also work hard to learn how to make others more receptive to being led in productive ways.

Jesus details a number of ways in which apparently good seed, or well-intentioned leadership, can fail to take root, each of which must be accounted for by those who would like to make the most of their potential as leaders. In this latter passage, of course, Jesus is quite clearly speaking of his own experience and work as a leader, even while his audience is made up of those he aims to lead.

The other lesson is a more general one. It is not enough to merely act, even in ways that are broadly and rightly thought to be productive. The most effective leaders leave nothing to chance, instead always seeking to prepare the ground for their activities that will follow. They engage in and engage others in the hard work of tilling the figurative soil that will support their efforts that follow, coupling their energy and drive with a commitment to acting strategically and focusing on the ultimate goal.

Lesson 7: Leave Nothing Behind Until It is Truly Lost

As strategic a leader as any, Jesus constantly reminds his followers and all who will listen not to give in to surface temptations and to instead look deeper.

Throughout the New Testament, Jesus teaches not just those who might be thought of as being best positioned to hear him, but a broad selection of people, including many whom society in general had condemned and cast out.

As a leader, then, Jesus understands that giving up at the first sign of trouble is not an option. No leader can afford to dwell unduly on true failure, but, at the same time, it is important to resist the urge to close the door on a situation just when things seem to have taken a turn for the worse. Jesus makes this point a number of times throughout the Gospels, perhaps most tellingly in this passage from Luke:

> *Or suppose a woman has ten silver coins and loses one. Doesn't she light a lamp, sweep the house and search carefully until she finds it? And when she finds it, she calls her friends and neighbors together and says, 'Rejoice with me; I have found my lost coin.'* (Luke 15: 8-9, NIV)

With nine coins still in hand, the woman might be expected to be content with having lost one, just as a leader of today might be encouraged to give up on a project of relatively minor significance that seems to be lost. Jesus instead encourages his listeners that, whatever bounty they might feel they are left with; they should make a real effort to track down something that has been lost.

Jesus himself does the same in his ministry, working at least as hard to enlighten the lost and condemned of society as he does to sway those who are already deemed worthy. In a time of endemic cost-cutting and obsessive drive toward efficiency, it can be tempting as a leader to do the opposite, to give up on people and projects as soon as they seem to have been lost. As Jesus makes clear in an analogous passage in the Gospel of Matthew, though, this premature condemnation can close off real opportunities:

> *What do you think? If a man owns a hundred sheep, and one of them wanders away, will he not leave the ninety-nine on the hills and go to look for the one that wandered off? And if he finds it, truly I tell you, he is happier about that one sheep than about the ninety-nine that did not wander off.* (Matt. 18: 12-13, NIV)

In working to salvage things, to track down and restore what has seemingly be lost, leaders and their subordinates can not only end up tangibly richer, like the woman who lost a silver coin, but also better off in terms of having learned from their experiences. As one of history's greatest and most dedicated leaders himself, Jesus embodied this teaching, working just as hard to save the seemingly doomed as those who had no such burdens. Leaders who strive to embody this lesson themselves will grow as a result, becoming more effective for the effort.

Lesson 8: Appeal to More than Greed

Modern leadership and management mores tend toward the material, rightly recognizing that providing subordinates with worthwhile incentives is an effective way of motivating them to do good work. Made explicit in the form of reinforcement theory and equity theory, this outlook ultimately drives many of today's organizations. While this carrot-and-stick approach is likely to be an important part of any capable leader's toolbox, it is not the end of the story.

In fact, working to foster commitment and personal investment among employees or subordinates can be just as important, and it is an approach that is frequently neglected today. With so many organizations coming to think of employees as essentially disposable or interchangeable, it is only natural to think that such efforts are likely to meet with skepticism, but the truth is that feelings of loyalty and involvement remain as powerful as ever.

Jesus makes this point aptly in a lesser-known parable from the Gospel of Matthew. The Kingdom of Heaven, he says,

> *is like a landowner who went out early in the morning to hire laborers for his vineyard. After*

agreeing with the laborers for the usual daily wage, he sent them into his vineyard. When he went out about nine o'clock he saw others standing idle in the marketplace and he said to them, "You also go into the vineyard, and I will pay you whatever is right." So they went. When he went out again about noon and about three o'clock, he did the same. And about five o'clock he went out and found others standing around and he said to them, "Why are you standing here idle all day?" They said to him, "Because no one has hired us." He said to them, "You also go into the vineyard." When evening came, the owner of the vineyard said to his manager, "Call the laborers and give them their pay, beginning with the last and then going to the first." When those hired about five o'clock came, each of them received the usual daily wage. Now when the first came, they thought they would receive more but each of them also received the usual daily wage. And when they received it, they grumbled against the land-owner, saying, "These last worked only one hour, and you have made them equal to us who have borne the burden of the day and the scorching heat." But he replied to one of them, "Friend, I am doing you no wrong; did you not agree with me for the usual daily wage? Take what belongs to you and go; I choose to give to

this last the same as I give to you. Am I not
allowed to do what I choose with what belongs to
me? Or are you envious because I am generous?"
(Matt 20: 1-15, NIV)

A leader who was committed solely to the transactional approach that is so common in the modern business world would have paid every worker according to how many hours that person worked that day. The Kingdom of Heaven, Jesus says, is not like this; while these material considerations have their place, they are not the sum total of what matters, despite what some might think.

By taking a broader view that still respects the material side of things, shortchanging nobody, the landowner who represents the Kingdom of Heaven in this parable is working to create a more resilient, reliable organization. Instead of allowing people to become entirely focused on their own personal interests, a kind of devolution that can just as well become destructive in a modern organization as it can be helpful, he shakes things up with an unexpected bit of generosity.

Deviating from the usual *quid pro quo* relationship between employer and hired help, Jesus is explaining, helps to build commitment among all. The landowner in the parable gave everyone their due and then some, thereby layering a new dimension onto the relationship that can only help in the future. As Jesus suggests with this story, truly effective leaders need to be able to hold their most valued tools, in this case proven motivational techniques, up to the same kind of scrutiny that they habitually apply to themselves and their subordinates.

Lesson 9: Spread the word

Although he was almost constantly exhorting his disciples and audiences to focus on examining and perfecting themselves instead of pursuing worldly fame and fortune, Jesus was anything but a retiring person. He actively put himself in front of all who would listen to him, seeking to spread his message as far and successfully as possible before he was called away.

In his best-known speech of all, the Sermon on the Mount, Jesus makes it plain that, despite the apparent nature of much of his advice, he did not at all mean that people had a duty to retreat from the world. To the contrary, he insisted to the entire gathered crowd, perhaps the largest of his ministry, that

> You are the light of the world. A town built on a hill cannot be hidden. Neither do people light a lamp and put it under a bowl. Instead they put it on its stand, and it gives light to everyone in the house. In the same way, let your light shine before others, that they may see your good deeds and

glorify your Father in heaven. (Matt. 5: 14-16, NIV)

This pointed lesson, of course, was not delivered in isolation. It is posed in the famous context of the Beatitudes, a moving sequence that begins "Blessed are the poor in spirit, for theirs is the kingdom of heaven." On the one hand, then, Jesus begins the Sermon on the Mount by upending the usual relationships of power on Earth. On the other hand, he also demands that the members of his audience should not shy from influencing others, particularly in terms of the positive example they set.

Far from being one dimensional, then, Jesus' teachings of this and other sorts form a whole that very much accounts for the realities of the world. Those who seek to become better leaders by learning from his teachings are not to take away the idea that all Jesus has to offer is lessons about the importance of humility, self-improvement, and empathizing with the powerless.

Jesus instead points out that those who undertake the difficult tasks he sets before them have a further responsibility: to let their "light shine before others." Addressing an entire crowd of people "from Galilee, the Decapolis, Jerusalem, Judea and the region across the Jordan," Jesus compels them all to be leaders, to let their hard work inspire others to greater things.

If many of Jesus' lessons can be difficult for leaders and those in positions of power to accept at first, this one is likely much less so. It is important to remember, though, that Jesus also condemns empty, reflexive, unthinking displays of authority and power; when he tells the gathered crowd to let their light shine, he does so in the context of the difficult work he has set before them. Having committed to and followed through with such a radical, fundamental questioning of one's convictions, though, leaders should feel just as compelled to set an example for others and spread the word to anybody willing to listen.

Lesson 10: Live the Golden Rule
If Jesus is known throughout the world today for a single idea, it is undoubtedly the Golden Rule. In fact, he himself posed the notion as a summation of his extensive, wide-ranging teachings, finding that it perfectly encapsulated everything he was called upon to communicate to others:

> *So in everything, do to others what you would have them do to you, for this sums up the Law and the Prophets.* (Matt. 7: 12, NIV)

Rarely in human history has a single concept been so influential and enduring. The Golden Rule is still today, thousands of years later, one of the single most frequently referred to teachings of all, finding its way into everything from the many corners of popular culture to the esoteric philosophy of Immanuel Kant.

It can also be a strikingly difficult precept to live up to. This is especially true for those who find themselves in positions of power and influence, where the likelihood of receiving in turn the kind of treatment that is doled out to less powerful people can often seem remote.

The point of the Golden Rule, however, is not about the immediate repercussions of treating others with a lack of empathy or compassion. In line with Jesus' many teachings, it is instead a lesson about how treating others badly can in and of itself diminish the person who acts so.

In a time when pragmatism and ruthlessness can seem to rule all, it can be hard to accept a notion like the Golden Rule and to give it its proper due. One thing that is certain, though, is that those leaders whom history judges most favorably not only held power over people, they were also invariably equipped with moral groundings that allowed them to overcome the urge to abuse that power.

The Golden Rule, then, serves as a perfect check on what can be an overwhelming temptation to think of other human beings as mere ends toward a goal. Of all of the spiritual teachings in human history, it is likely one of the most powerfully succinct of all, and therefore one that leaders of every sort can do well to become comfortable and familiar with.

CONCLUSION

Jesus was an incredibly complex figure, with the ultimate clarity of his messages often being couched in surprising and even contradictory-seeming language and delivery. As a leader, Jesus was undoubtedly one of the most creative and resourceful of all, giving birth to a wealth of images, parables, and sayings that seem every bit as vital today as they must have to his audiences of the time.

There are also a number of common themes that run throughout his teachings and that are expressed in the methods by which he taught, and today's leaders are just as well advised to take note of these as they are of the concrete lessons themselves. One of the most striking of these, of course, is that prevailing arrangements and convictions, however set in stone they might seem to be and whatever form they might take, are always to be questioned.

At times, Jesus promises concrete rewards for those who succeed in this endeavor, although it seems more likely that, in general, he was interested in upsetting the status quo for the personal development it could provoke in his disciples. It should be clear, though, that modern leaders who wish to learn from Jesus should adopt the same restless, never-satisfied outlook that he consistently encourages, whether that means striving to improve the performance of their less-remarkable subordinates, or continually striving to become better people themselves.

Another important current of Jesus' teaching that is especially important for today's leaders reveals itself in the methods he chose for leading others. Jesus, after all, was concerned not only with helping his disciples and others to become better people, but also with making his disciples into strong, persuasive leaders themselves.

Towards that end, he was both incredibly patient and uncommonly demanding, asking everything from his disciples that they could possibly give and supporting and encouraging them throughout. This can be the most difficult kind of balance of all for any leader to strike, as expediency and human nature both often seem determined to upset the scale one way or another. In the end, it is only through the humility and self-discipline that Jesus continually insists upon that anyone can hope to reach this pinnacle of the art of leadership.

BOOKS FROM MICHAEL WINICOTT

Another titles by Michael Winicott you may find interesting:

BILL GATES: BUSINESS LESSONS

BRAIN: EXERCISES TO EMPOWER

BUSINESS PLAN: A practical guide

FACEBOOK MARKETING: Business Lessons from Mark Zuckerberg

HABITS: MICRO CHANGES for MACRO RESULTS

HENRY FORD: ENTERPRENEURSHIP LESSONS

LEONARDO DA VINCI: CREATIVITY LESSONS

MARTIN LUTHER KING: LIFE LESSONS

OPRAH WINFREY: LIFE LESSONS

STEVE JOBS: BUSINESS LESSONS

WALT DISNEY: CREATIVITY LESSONS

WINSTON CHURCHILL: LEADERSHIP LESSONS

DID YOU ENJOY THIS BOOK?

Thanks for purchasing and reading this book. If you reached this page you had probably enjoyed this book. Would you care to leave a positive review in Amazon?

This is very important for 2 reasons:

a) I need your feedback to improve the quality of my books

b) Other people may read and benefit from this book if you share your thoughts.

 Thanks a lot for your review!

Michael Winicott

www.ingramcontent.com/pod-product-compliance
Lightning Source LLC
Chambersburg PA
CBHW071548170526
45166CB00004B/1590